Leaves

Lynn Stone

Rourke

Publishing LLC

Vero Beach, Florida 32964

www.rourkepublishing.com

PHOTO CREDITS: All photos © Lynn M. Stone, except pg.4 © Clayton Hansec; pg.6 © Malcolm Romai; pg. 9 © Jasenka Luska; pg.10 © Gina Goforth; pg.11, 15 © Stefan Klein; pg.12a © Jan Rihak; pg.12b © Andres Reh; pg.14 © Rebecca Paul; pg.16 © Lars Lindblad; pg.19 © Juan Estey; pg.21 © Angelafoto.

Editor: Robert Stengard-Olliges

Cover design by: Nicola Stratford, bdpublishing.com

Library of Congress Cataloging-in-Publication Data

Stone, Lynn M.
  Leaves / Lynn Stone.
    p. cm. -- (Plant parts)
  ISBN 978-1-60044-553-8 (Hardcover)
  ISBN 978-1-60044-693-1 (Softcover)
  1. Leaves--Juvenile literature. I. Title.
  QK649.S86 2008
  581.4'8--dc22
                              2007015155

Printed in the USA

CG/CG

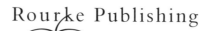

Rourke Publishing

www.rourkepublishing.com – rourke@rourkepublishing.com
Post Office Box 3328, Vero Beach, FL 32964

Table of Contents

Leaves Make Food

Just like you,
plants have to eat
to survive. And that's
one reason plants have
leaves. Leaves make plant food.
Think of leaves as a
plant's kitchen.

Photosynthesis is how plants make food. Photosynthesis happens in plants when sunlight, **carbon dioxide**, and water come together.

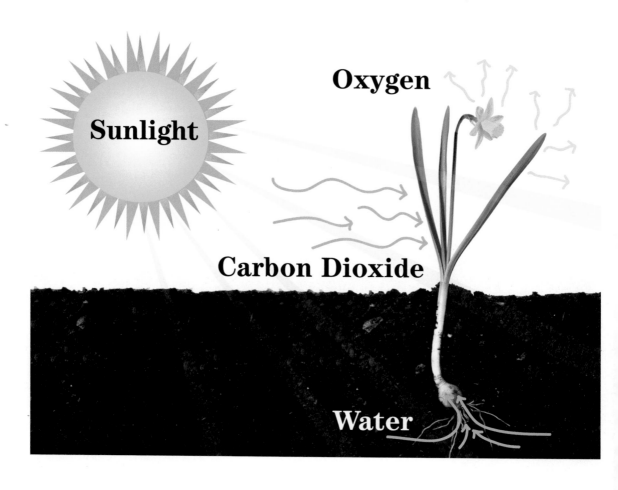

Oxygen

Sunlight

Carbon Dioxide

Water

Using the sun's energy, photosynthesis makes plant sugars. Most plants use these sugars as food.

Leaves have tiny openings. Leaves can capture and release air and water. Photosynthesis releases **oxygen** into the air.

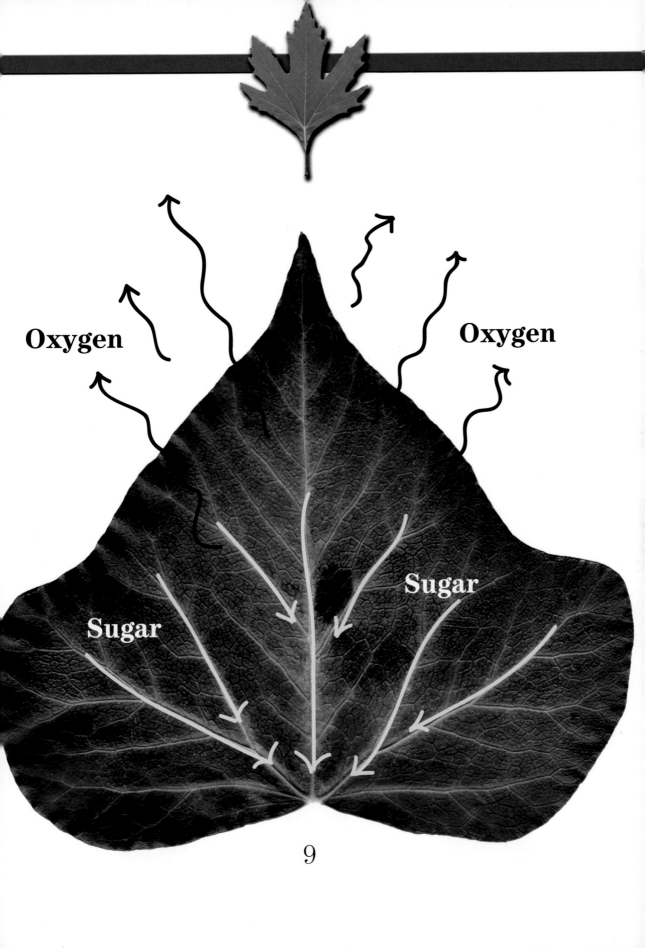

Oxygen

Oxygen

Sugar

Sugar

9

Different Leaves

Large and small plants grow leaves. Leaves grow from the stems of flowers. Leaves also grow from the branches of trees. There are many different leaves.

11

Leaves grow in many shapes and sizes. Grape leaves are big and wide. Ferns have many tiny leaves. The leaves of pine trees look like needles. They have sharp points too!

Fern Leaf

Grape Leaf

Pine Leaf

13

Some leaves are very simple. A maple tree leaf, for example, is a single leaf connected to a stem. Clovers have a few smaller leaves connected to the stem.

Maple

Clover

Leaves are usually green. Each fall, some leaves change color. That is because they no longer make food and green **chlorophyll**. Chlorophyll gives leaves their green color.

16

17

Leaves for Health

Look closely at a wide leaf. Notice the veins in it. Your veins carry blood. A leaf's veins carry water and other healthy things called **nutrients**.

Leaves look simple, but they do amazing work. Leaves are good for plants and people. We count on leaves for oxygen and food. Have you munched on lettuce, cabbage, or spinach lately?

Glossary

carbon dioxide (KAR buhn dye OK side) — an invisible gas in the air

chlorophyll (KLOR uh fil) — the green coloring made by plants

nutrients (NOO tree uhntz) — something that is nourishing, healthy

oxygen (OK suh juhn) — an invisible gas that plants and animals breathe

photosynthesis (foh toh SIN thuh siss) — how plants make food

Index

Further Reading

Bodach, Vijaya and Saunders-Smith, Gail. *Leaves*.
  Capstone Press, 2006.

Farndon, John. *Leaves*. Thomson Gale, 2006.

Thomson, Ruth. *Leaves*. Chrysalis Education, 2006.

Websites to Visit

www.kathimitchell.com/plants.html

www.picadome.fcps.net/lab/currl/plants/default.htm

About the Author

Lynn M. Stone is the author of more than 400 children's books. He is a talented natural history photographer as well. Lynn, a former teacher, travels worldwide to photograph wildlife in its natural habitat.